Remembrances & R...
By Two
Daughters of Guyana

Authors: Claire Martin Combs & Paula Matthews Hazlewood
Illustrated by: Elsa Harper & Paula Matthews Hazlewood

To order additional copies of this book, contact:
Xlibris Corporation
1-888-795-4274
www.Xlibris.com
Orders@Xlibris.com

Table of Contents

Conclusion
Scenes of Guyana
Song: Born in the Land of the Mighty Roraima

Acknowledgements

We are privileged to thank many people who made this book possible.

Cynthia Brower came into our project and became our agent. To her we say thanks for giving and leading us through the arduous process of publishing. Her sense of humor and her knowledge gave us confidence that the work would be completed.

We thank Aunt Rene Willock and her daughter Marcelle Willock, Leila Foster Mongul, and Late Aunt Una Matthews (Paula's Mother) for encouraging us at the inception of the project, and who permitted us to use their quotes in the text.

We are grateful to Christopher Martin for the numerous telephone calls he responded to with sound advice and humor, and the effort he put forward searching for and locating old photographs; thanks as well to his wife Anita Hotchkiss Martin for her reading and comments of encouragement.

Tony Martin and his wife Ruth Harry Martin for their suggestions, recipe reviews and corrections are appreciated and thanked.

Elsa Harper is recognized and thanked for her taking time from her busy schedule to contribute artwork.

We are grateful to Dmitri Gibbs for his advice and technical skills in setting up the cover design.

Beatrice London who was the first to see the rough draft and made positive comments and suggestions is thanked.

Dr. Marvin Dulaney of Avery Research Center, Charleston, South Carolina is thanked for his interest and suggestions for the project.

Megan Gibbs we give sincere thanks for the time and efficiency with which she proof read the text.

Our deepest love and gratitude go to our husbands, Ingram Hazlewood and Sam Combs. To Sam we are indebted for the patience he showed, the technical skills he used for the reproduction of pictures, the assembling of material and the long hours he put in to see this work completed to our satisfaction. Ingram is thanked for numerous suggestions, reading and rereading the text, making incidental corrections and encouraging us. Their patience during the writing of this book will always be remembered by us.

To all of the above we thank you for your love.

PROLOGUE

Conjuring up the Past
Claire & Paula

It was a cool, sunshiny autumn afternoon in New England. The sky was clear, the kind of day that invited reminiscences. Claire and I took the opportunity to drive up and attend a special art exhibit at Yale University in New Haven, Connecticut. After a few hours we emerged from that interesting show, and decided it was time for a snack.

We wandered down the narrow street and chose a small café. Its checkered tablecloths reminded us of our college days in other small towns, as well as the checkered oilcloth, often used in kitchens and pantry areas of our childhood homes. We opened the menu and were immediately pleased by the offering of tea and buttered scones. Almost simultaneously we chose tea, scones, cream and marmalade. As we waited, we were transported to a vividly remembered time when we, in our childhood and young adulthood, shared many teas, and helped to serve at formal tea parties.

We took a trip down Memory Lane. It was amazing how gratifying memories can become. We shared tales of holidays, our friends and just about being Guyanese youth in an era when the country was still under British rule and known as British Guiana.

The day drew to a close, evening approached and we returned to the car and began the three-hour ride back to New York City. We discussed the exhibit we had seen and then our chatter returned to "home, our native land, Guyana."

We came to the realization that we had so many tales we wanted others to hear. The idea of writing a book emerged. At first it was jokingly accepted. Later it became realistic. We concluded, "well we are literate and can certainly write our tales." We convinced ourselves, without too much effort, to embark on the project.

Our primary purpose, we felt was to inform our descendants of the kind of life we shared as we grew up. We also wanted to give other people a glimpse of life in that part of the world called British Guiana in the '40s and '50s. By the time we got to NYC, we had pledged to write our book.

We had several meetings about how to relate our story. It became obvious that since we kept bringing up the food we ate that we should tell our story through the holidays in Guyana and connect them to the unique recipes used on those days. We set sail on this voyage, and invite you to join us.

Chapter I

We're going to tell you a Story
Claire & Paula

After many years away from "home" we find ourselves reminiscing and spicing our conversations more and more about "home." We mean no disrespect to our adopted country, for we made the choice to remain in the United States of America as citizens of this great country. However, we have chosen to celebrate the place of our birth by recalling our growing-up years in British Guiana, the El Dorado of Sir Walter Raleigh. The United States of America has been kind to us and we are glad this is your birth home and our chosen home.

Over these many years, you children in both our families have heard us say countless times, *"if only these children had our childhood"* or *"now-a-days children are not like us when we were growing up."* You, the younger generation, have in turn asked, *"what is so different?"* or *"what, do you mean you had nannies?"* and *"what did she mean about having a "Que-que?"* (an African dance), or *"how come Claire is your country cousin and not just a cousin?"*

We decided to recount for you children, grandchildren, nephews, great-nephews and great-nieces, explanations to some of these questions. We wish you to follow us into the realm of our childhood and young adulthood of our day. So come along. Let us take you on a journey through a typical year of activities that were important to us, as kids growing up in a British colonial country in South America called British Guiana. The years we speak of are from the 1940s through the 1950s.

There are a few things we would like

Children of Guyana

you to know about the society and culture in British Guiana, before it became the Republic of Guyana in 1966. The society was divided not by race but by class. There were six racially different groups of people in British Guiana. These included native Amerindians, Indians from East Asia, Portuguese, Chinese, descendants of Africans, and white expatriates, generally from the United Kingdom, who, depending on their class, mixed rather well.

We all lived together not in segregated housing areas. We shared what was a colonial class structure based on education, occupation and ancestry. This structure resulted in an upper and upper-middle class dominated by British Colonial Government officials, managers of large rice and sugar estates, professionals such as doctors and lawyers, ministers of religion, headmasters and headmistresses of private educational institutions. The middle class included schoolteachers, nurses, bank personnel, colonial government employees as well as owners of businesses, merchants and owners of real estate. The lower class was made up of persons who were domestic servants, laborers on sugar estates, and those who could not afford a certain standard of living but worked hard and sent their children to school.

The class structure crossed all racial, ethnic lines and religious groups, resulting in a population that was more conscious of class than ethnicity. Nevertheless, it was always possible for persons to move up in society through education, economics, perseverance and good fortune.

As you read our stories you will find references to servants. Both of our families were members of the upper and middle classes and had the means to employ domestic servants, most of whom were African descendants like us. They made up an invaluable part of the society that nurtured us.

We hope that these observations will clarify some of our references as you read our story.

Chapter II

Our Ancestors came from across The Seas
Paula & Claire

The Matthews-Hendricks Connection - Paula

My Dear Sons:

As you begin to have your own families and move away from home in pursuit of your own destinies, I thought this an excellent time to communicate in writing what you have heard about your Guyanese heritage. What I will write will give you a record of our youth and the cultural climate in which we were reared. I hope that these writings along with Claire's letter to her nephews and nieces will give you a reference from which to tell your descendants about your forefathers.

Our friends and I have discovered that as we grow older it is so easy to look into the past and perceive those days as the *"good old days."* We may fool ourselves sometimes, but we will not have any doubt that our childhood in British Guiana in the 1940s and 1950s was one colorful and beautiful experience.

It was then and there that we learned the moral codes and ethical values by which we try to live, and by example, share with you. These tenets are all a part of your genealogy and spiritual heritage. They are derived from both sides of your family, maternal and paternal.

Reverends Patrick and Una Matthews

On both my mother's and my father's side there are individuals who worked hard, served their communities and were recognized as achievers. My mother's father, Joseph Hyll Hendricks, and her grandfather, F.C. Glasgow, were ministers in the Congregational denomination. Mrs. Hendricks, your great grandmother, was a qualified midwife and health visitor. My mother is one of 11 Hendricks children. You will remember best Uncle Leslie Hendricks. The Glasgow–Hendricks families were descendants of African slaves who later became freemen and women and owned land in Beterverwagting, East Coast, Demerara.

On granddad Matthews' side of the family the genealogical picture is different. The original Matthews ancestor in Guyana was an Englishman who was a teacher in the Essequibo River region. He married a native Guyanese, and their descendants married other natives including Aboriginal Indians as well as some persons from French Guiana. These people were mainly businessmen who owned large parcels of land, and they soon entered the lumber industry.

My father was an Ordained Minister. He received all of his secondary education and graduate training in religion, in England in the 1920s. He was a superb orator and his parishioners listened to him with delight.

As a child, one of my first wishes was to have a voice and bearing like my father. I imitated him as best I could even though I never thought of being a minister. My mother, Una Inez Glasgow Hendricks, was a tireless social worker, a pioneer among women in the communications field. She was a newspaper reporter and was a radio show host. She traveled widely to foreign countries with my father.

She came to New York City, graduated from New York Theological Seminary and was ordained. She returned to Guyana and pastored the Congrerational Church at Mission Chapel, New Amsterdam.

Marco and I dressed in our school uniforms; his Queen's College, mine Bishops' High School

When she relocated to live permanently in the USA, she contributed as a Supply Minister for the United Church of Christ and founded Guyanese United Church Women in America.

It is from her that I learned the code of service to others and to make the best of whatever circumstances one encounters.

One of the glaring differences between your childhood and mine was the fact that we were not aware or concerned with the *"question of color."* Remember that my dad was light skinned and Mom was very dark. We have cousins who run the gamut of color and hair texture from white to very dark skinned people, from kinky hair to satiny silk hair. Many of our relatives were considered Portuguese since they married Portuguese spouses, and some were considered East Indian. But as children we never noticed those differences. We took it all for granted that cousins could be any shade.

My brother Marc and I were exposed to many visitors from the London Missionary Society and other English visitors who stayed in our home, became friends and were called Aunt Flo and Uncle Bill or whatever their names. This was not strange to us since we were taught that as a courtesy, we referred to our parents' friends with those terms of endearment and respect. We therefore experienced positive relationships with all people.

It was not until I arrived in the USA, at the age of 20, to attend Wellesley College in Massachusetts, that I was confronted with the idea that there was something inherently different between people of white skin and those of black skin.

I have never accepted that theory. I hope that I have passed on the assurance to you that the color of one's skin does *"not make the man,"* and that we as dark-skinned people are equal in *"humanness"* to anyone. The color of our skin, I believe, is no indication, prediction or measure of one's success. We had been brought up to consider ourselves equal to all people, no matter what their skin color. We were taught that all status in life carried various responsibilities to yourself and to your community. My father, as a minister, set the example for us by showing respect and honor to all our neighbors. This tenet may account for my success as a teacher and the ease of my interpersonal relationships wherever I have dwelt.

A Buxton House

Most of my early childhood was spent in Buxton, a village on the East Coast of the Demerara River. It is twelve miles from Georgetown, the capital city. Later, as my dad was reassigned, we moved to Georgetown, then to the Corentyne coast and back to Georgetown, where I lived until I departed for the United States in 1953.

So with this capsule of Glasgow-Hendricks-Matthews family let us go on to the holidays and the foods we enjoyed in British Guiana, *"The El Dorado of South America."*

Claire P. Martin-Combs, with whom I write this book, has been a personal friend and a *"country cousin"* since our early childhood. Our parents were friends before we were born. Claire's mother, Aunt Ruby, baked and decorated my mother's wedding cake in 1932. Aunt Ruby was a wonderful lady, a well-trained caterer, a businesswoman, a teacher, and a woman of indefatigable energy and humor. You will hear more about her from Claire's remembrances.

Lovingly, Mom (Paula)

My mother's wedding cake made by Aunt Ruby

Claire

The Martin-Donavan Connection
Guyana - Barbados

My Dear Nephews & Nieces:

To appreciate this book of our remembrances of holidays and food, you need to know that for my brothers and me, growing up in British Guiana was really wonderful.

As of this writing, it is 48 years now that I have called the United States of America "home", and I am very happy here. Growing up in another country and living under a different culture is part of my make-up. I want you to know about this so that you know your ancestry and the country of your fathers, grandfathers and grandmothers before British Guiana became independent of Great Britain in 1966 and became the Republic called "Guyana."

Christopher and Anthony in their scout uniforms
Claire's Brothers

In the 1940s and 1950s, life for my brothers and me was uncomplicated by politics. Our focus was to follow the directions of our parents, enjoy our friends and family, and study hard. We were being groomed to study abroad, to further our education and become professionally trained in the fields of engineering and health care management, which we all achieved.

Our childhood was family-centered with an emphasis on learning, nurturing friendships, the theater and adventure. Your fathers and I were born in the city of Georgetown, which to this day is the capital of the country. You may remember from your geography classes in school that British Guiana is on the northeastern coast of the continent of South America. Our neighbor to the west is Venezuela, Brazil lies to the south, Dutch Guiana (now called Surinam), to the east, and the vast Atlantic Ocean our northern boundary. We had very little contact with our South American neighbors, who spoke Spanish, Portuguese and Dutch respectively, because we were the only English-speaking country on the continent at that time.

What we did have was a rich culture reflective of our historic settlement, for British Guiana was and is a multiracial, multiethnic country with Amerindian, African, Caucasian, East Indian, Portuguese and Chinese peoples. As the races intermarried, we developed many mixtures that included Guyanese mulatto, santantone, and dougla' peoples, who were offspring of white and African, Portuguese and African, and East Indian and African ancestry respectively.

The Martin family history includes the descendants of African slaves, English, Irish and Dutch colonial settlers and German traders. The African and English heritages go back to the 18th century, the Irish, Dutch and German to the 19th century. These diverse ethnic ancestors were independent thinkers. They carved out their economic stability by becoming business people, professionals, government employees, and members of the local middle–class intelligentsia.

My Great- Grandmother Ma Donavon

The Irish branch of the family history boasts a titled ancestor, on whose plantation on the island of Barbados, your paternal great great-grandmother and your great grandmother were born. Family history has it that your great-great grandmother was disowned, and exiled in the 1870's for consorting with a free man of color and having his child, Constance, your great grandmother. As a result, your great great–grandmother left Barbados and came to British Guiana where she married and had three more daughters, Elizabeth, Olive and Clarise. These were our ancestors on my father's side. Constance was her oldest daughter, a strong and determined woman who did not allow the stigma of her birth to influence her ambitions or diminish her respect in the community. She married and became a midwife.

Her son was my father, Alexander Adolphus Donovan Martin. He was known as A.A.D. Martin or Bertie Martin. We children never could understand where "Bertie" came from.

Our Dad was a highly intelligent man of strong opinions. He was also an anglophile, who, contrariwise, battled against the British colonial rulers and their stereotypical (low) expectations of the local population. He constantly challenged these expectations and suffered for it.

Dad was a career colonial government official whose contribution in his official capacity was the implementation of a nutrition program for children who lived in the "interior" or equatorial jungle.

His passion and signature contribution to the Guyanese culture, however, was the expansion of The Theater Guild, where he produced and directed plays for the stage and radio. He also trained actors and was a riveting speaker. He has been published in the Kyk–over–Al, a journal of intellectual essays, opinions and editorials by writers of the West Indies. He was also a teacher.

Circa 1911 – My Grandparents, Conrad and Constance Martin with my Father, Alexander Adolphus Donovan Martin, and his younger Sister, Iris Martin, Georgetown, British, Guiana

In the early 1950s Dad was accepted to study theater production at the Bristol Old Vic in Bristol, England, -famous for training Sir Lawrence Olivier and other Shakespearean actors. My brothers and I were sometimes involved in our father's productions.

Dad's father, Conrad Martin, was of mixed race and worked as a pattern maker on the rice plantations. He was born at Rose Hall in the Corentyne region. His work involved the creation of patterns for machines and their parts. He was also a businessman from the late 1890s until he died in the 1940s in his seventies. I remember him still.

Our mother, Ruby Edith Camella Pollard Martin, was a well-known caterer, teacher and former Manager and Housekeeper of the British Colonial Government House from the 1920s, under at least 2 British colonial Governors. She was born in Georgetown in 1899 to Julia Pollard, who was of mixed race, and Herr Speight, a German Jew. He was the local representative of the gold syndicate who mined and exported gold in the 1880–1890s. He died of black-water fever in the early 1900s. This is a very serious illness caused from an insect bite (probably a mosquito) in the deep jungle where the gold was mined.

My Mother and Father in Canada - 1947

Our mother showed an early creative skill in the art of cooking and her mother agreed that she should be apprenticed to an American woman, Mrs. Jordan, an expatriate businesswoman, who was the leading caterer in British Guiana in the early 1900s. It was this training that prepared her for her role as the Manager and Housekeeper of the British Colonial Governor's residence and later as a teacher of domestic science at the Carnegie Trade Center in Georgetown.

Food was an important part of our lives, particularly because of our mother's profession. As children we developed fine palates and appreciation for excellent cuisine and formal dining that derived from the generations of the diverse cultures of our country and our ancestry. This is our heritage. Paula and I will share these grand experiences with you as we remember. We will take you through a typical year of feasts, holidays and family gatherings and share with you the rich cuisine that reflects the various dishes of the Guyanese traditions. Read for some more of our good times.

Ruby Pollard circa 1925

Chapter III

Father Christmas is coming to Town
Paula & Claire

After some discussion we decided to begin our year with you on Christmas. We felt that Christmas was the most loved holiday in Guyana and the one that Guyanese everywhere recreate annually, no matter where they may live.

We fashioned a questionnaire and distributed it to some of our friends to see if our sentiments were valid. Imagine our joy at the enthusiasm they expressed for the Christmas holiday. There was overwhelming support for Christmas as the most loved holiday in Guyana.

Leila Foster Mongul, a close friend of Claire's from her school days, wrote, "Christmas was naturally the best holiday for us children. Carol singing, gifts and specially made treats created by my mother. Ginger beer...made in those days from dried gingerroot and left to ripen for a few days; Fly, made from potatoes...a light refreshing drink; garlic pork being prepared three days before Christmas and eaten with aniseed bread on Christmas morning. All of these foods were a gastronomic delight. I remember riding my bicycle home from 7a.m. church service along our main street and smelling nothing but

JOYS OF CHRISTMAS

Oh, Little Town of Bethlehem
How still we see thee lie!
Above thy deep and dreamless sleep
The silent stars go by:
Yet in the dark streets shineth the everlasting light.
The hopes and fears of all the years
Are met in thee tonight.

garlic pork being prepared all the way home. There were also different types of cakes made, but the 'piece de resistance' was Guyanese Black Cake." Heartened by these responses Paula will now tell you about her happy memories.

This well-known Christmas carol, Oh Little Town of Bethlehem and ones like it evoked instant memories of an unforgettable time.

Buxton Congregational Church Manse c 1940
(Sketch by Paula)

Paula's Recollections

The best Christmases I spent were between the ages of four and eleven, when we lived at Buxton Congregational Manse. Buxton is a village on the East Coast of the Demerara River, founded by freed slaves. After the Emancipation Proclamation in 1834, through the hard work of these freed black families, the village developed primarily as an agricultural area. Here too evolved post-emancipation village government in British Guiana.

Christmas in Buxton was the reflection of heaven for my brother and me. Bring your imagination and just savor what it was like in the 1930s and 1940s as we lived our youth.

An air of anticipation began to build right after harvest in November, about which you will hear later. My mother started her annual preparations early in December. She first made lots of lists. Of these many lists, one related to her personal tasks, one for the household help and one to each member of the family.

She distributed the lists to each person and the recipient then decided how to carry out his or her chores. It seemed the biggest one was shopping. My Dad took the family into the capital city, Georgetown, for dinner. Dessert was from "Brown Betty," the first ice-cream parlor opened in Guyana. We then went window-shopping. What glee we had in seeing all the tiny colored lights, toys and books and gifts in those windows! Looking at the windows made my heart race madly. I imagined what presents I would receive as Christmas gifts.

A few days after this trip, my parents left for their own shopping day in Georgetown. They returned laden with goodies like imported ham wrapped in black sticky wax paper, pounds and pounds of dried fruits to make Guyanese black cake. All were carefully stored after our cook's inspection. At the sight of those items Marc and I became even more excited about these holidays. We thought of what we would give everyone and what we hoped to receive. The real bustle began in mid-December and the cook became the authority in the household. It was her job to coordinate all the efforts of the house help. She made sure that all the ingredients for every possible dish were on hand.

First she assembled and prepared the ingredients for the Christmas black cake and mincemeat pies. She directed the grinding of the dried fruits (prunes, raisins and currants), cinnamon and cloves; the mixture was put into a large earthenware jar and covered with wine and rum and left to age. I loved the smell of this mixture and would often sneak a taste if I were around when the cook tested it.

Guyana Black Cake Recipe

1-1/2 lbs. of dried fruit
2 oz. of mixed citrus peels
1 tsp. of mixed spices (cinnamon, allspice, and cloves)
4 oz. chopped walnuts or peanuts
8 oz. brown sugar
8 oz. margarine
6 eggs
1/4 tsp. baking powder
8 oz. flour sifted
1/2 bottle of port wine or rum
Make caramel from one lb. sugar & 2 Tbs. wine

Directions:

Wash & dry fruits, grind and add chopped nuts. Prepare caramel by heating the sugar with the wine until a dark color is reached. Lay aside. Mix the wine, rum, fruits and nuts and leave to soak in an earthenware jar for a week or longer. Using an eight-inch cake pan, grease and line pan (bottom and sides) with 2 layers of greaseproof baking paper. Put this aside, mix sugar and margarine well adding eggs one at a time until mixture is creamy. Now add mixture of fruits and nuts and fold in. Add sifted flour, baking powder and spices gradually and again fold into cake mixture. Add prepared caramel, a little at a time, to give required dark color to cake batter. Add remaining liquor from the fruit and nuts to make a soft flowing consistency. Pour this into the cake pan and bake in pre-heated oven of 300 degrees for 2-3 hours. Bake in the middle of the oven to promote even baking. Always test for doneness and firmness in middle of cake with a tooth-pick. When pick comes out dry it is done. Pour wine or rum over the cake and repeat over several days to keep cake moist.

This cake lasts for months if kept moist with the above. At about the same time, the preparation of garlic pork commenced. We thank the Portuguese immigrants for this delicious dish, which they contributed to the Guyanese cuisine.

Garlic Pork Recipe

1 lb. of lean pork loin
2 Tbs. fresh thyme leaves (include some stems)
1 head of garlic cloves, peeled, crushed & diced)
Salt to taste
Fresh hot pepper to taste, diced with seeds
White Vinegar

Directions:

Make sure the pork is thoroughly cleaned. Cut pork into bite sized pieces. Wash with lime or lemon juice. Set pork and other ingredients in a jar and cover with vinegar. Set aside to marinate at least five days until Christmas morning. When ready to cook, use a hardy frying pan. Add the mixture, retaining a few tablespoons of the marinade, to the frying pan. Cook covered over medium heat until most of the liquid has been reduced. Uncover and fry pork in its own oil as it browns. Add the retained marinade and simmer five minutes. Serve with hot boiled plantains or potatoes.

Amidst all the food preparations, the houseboy had his own chores. His main job was to remove all spider webs (so common in tropical countries) and dust from every nook and cranny, especially the ceilings. In order to do this he made *pointer brooms* from collected dead branches of the coconut tree. He stripped the fronds from their ribs and tied these remaining ribs together tightly to form flexible swish brooms. He tied one broom to a long stick and used that one to sweep the ceiling spaces too high to reach while standing on the floor. It was fun to see a pointer broom that Claire brought back from her last trip to Guyana in 1989. She still has it.

Two Coconut Trees in Center
(Sketch by Paula)

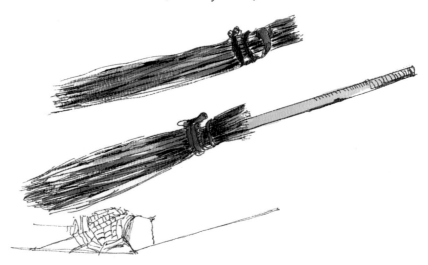

Handmade Pointer Broom
(Sketch by Paula)

The fun began. Our home was a hive of activity.

One fascinating custom was the purchase of new curtains and new linoleum.

About a week before Christmas a delivery van from Bookers, the leading store in the country, arrived. What had he brought? He delivered the linoleum, which my mother had chosen on her last trip to Georgetown. Judging from the number of rolls in his van, everyone in the village had brand new linoleum to be installed by Christmas. Ours was laid in the kitchen and in the bathroom, and possibly a strip along the gallery. In a little room off the kitchen, a sewing machine was set up and a local seamstress busied herself cutting and fashioning new curtains. There were no fancy machines in those days, only ones that sewed straight seams. Somehow or other, those curtains were finished by Christmas Eve and hung not a minute earlier than midnight.

On Christmas Eve, the kitchen was a vortex of activity and bustle. The maids, the cook and the hapless houseboy were all busy at their chores. The houseboy did all he could not to get in Cookie's (that was the name we called her) way. All the stoves were fired up, the coal pot smoldered and the kitchen sweltered from all the blazing fires and heat from the oven. Cookie lined up all the foods for Christmas Day. She knew just how long each item took to cook and when it would be served. Sometimes, alas, she discovered that there was not enough room to bake all the black cake. She would send the houseboy over to the local bakery shop to book a space for her pans of batter. He would return and tell her when the bakery could accommodate her pans. At the appointed time, she sent the pans by a trusted maid or took them herself. The black fruitcake, one of the symbols of Christmas, is still created for special occasions such as weddings, christenings, and significant birthdays and always at Christmas. It is the delicious rummy taste that I enjoyed and still enjoy. It is particularly rich in calories.

Christmas Eve Day was a day of confusion and great hubbub. It was the day on which our dad was ready to decorate the house and the tree. He always chose to use an English motif, which involved snow. Of course we children became creative. We sat and laboriously strung numerous lengths of thread through cotton balls to imitate snowflakes. We assembled them and hung the lengths from the ceiling beams. Dad was very good at festooning the entire gallery, which is the narrow enclosed area of the house at the head of the outside front stairs. It stretched across the full width of the home. The seating area usually faced the windows and the street. It was customary to sit and observe the passing scene, wave and hail friends as they passed by.

Homes Featuring Galleries (Georgetown)

The Christmas tree was a sturdy tree trunk stuck in a pot of sand and pebbles. Its branches were wire hangers covered with green crepe paper. There was an art to creating these "trees" and we spent several afternoons preparing them. Everything was assembled and the tree decorated. For decorations we used imported ornaments as well as items we created from magazine ideas.

Paula's family before their Christmas tree

Typical Handmade Xmas Tree
(Sketch by Paula)

By the time the tree was completed, our house was a virtual fairy-land. Dad was a jolly fellow, and it meant a great deal to him to have us enjoy Christmas. Sometimes he fashioned Santa Claus out of ice apples. These apples were imported in cold storage, hence the name ice apple, from the United Kingdom and abroad. He used cotton wool for the beard, cloves for the eyes, and then placed these figures in the center of the table surrounded by miniature gifts. I shall never forget Christmas with my Dad. Naturally he never let us forget whose birthday it was. We were "children of the Manse,"- the parsonage, and we revered the religious meaning of Christmas.

But being children, we always scoffed quietly about the saying, "it is better to give than to receive," since we thought the greatest thing was to receive our gifts, in spite of the wise men and the three Kings who came to celebrate Christ's birth.

Even in the present as I prepare my adult Christmas, I recall the wonderful scents that engulfed my childhood home. I do my best to recreate that special scent which is Christmas. On Christmas Eve the most dominant aroma was that of a special dish called "pepperpot" as it boiled up for the umpteenth time that day. It was at its best on Christmas morning. Its aroma mingled with that of the garlic pork and baked ham. What a meeting of fragrances! Our mouths watered for the morrow and all the traditional dishes, which would come forth from the kitchen for breakfast.

At about evening time on Christmas Eve our thoughts gravitated to the visit from Father Christmas and Christmas gifts. Carolers traditionally came by early in the evenings and sang in our home, crowded into the enclosed staircase and gallery. They performed familiar and beloved carols and we joined in for "We wish you a Merry Christmas."

Trays filled with cookies, fudge, and imported candies were served, accompanied by glasses of cool lemonade. Everyone had a snack. When I was old enough, I was allowed to make the fudge and this is the recipe I have followed all these years.

Paula's Fudge Recipe

2 cups sugar
2 tablespoons of cocoa or chocolate
2/3 cups evaporated or plain milk
2 tablespoons of butter or margarine
Pinch of salt
1-teaspoon vanilla or almond extract

Place sugar, chocolate, liquid, butter and pinch of salt in a pan. Heat over medium heat, stirring constantly until sugar is dissolved. Cover until the mixture begins to boil, remove cover and continue to boil on low heat. As mixture begins to thicken and clings to the spoon, take a few drops out and put onto a saucer of cold water. If these drops can be formed into a ball, then the fudge is almost ready. Remove pan from the stove, add the extract and let cool for a few minutes. Test again in cold water and if these drops did not make a ball, put back on low heat and boil a little longer. If too stiff then add a little milk and mix again. When satisfied that mixture is ready, pour into a well buttered dish and mark into squares. Remove when completely cooled.

Symbols of Christmas

The carolers departed, singing as they went, and my parents went to church at midnight. We children went to bed early and tried to sleep, but the excitement and anticipation made that difficult.

It seemed as though only a short time passed before the smells of garlic wafted up to my bedroom. Up I jumped and rushed to the living room. Sure enough, Santa Claus had come and gone. There were stockings brimming with toys and assorted packages nearby. The only thing I had to do was wait for my parents and my brother, Marc, to awaken. I rushed into the bedrooms and whispered semi-loudly, "Father Christmas was here." Eventually, everyone came into the living room and expressed many "Ooh and Ahs," at all the toys under the tree. The tinkling of a bell or the clanging of the gong summoned us to breakfast.

The sideboard was laden with such traditional foods as garlic pork, cassava bread, plantains, grapefruit halves, ice-apples, aniseed bread, plait bread, and codfish stew. You can see that this was a variety breakfast. In my family we ate and then distributed the personal gifts. We went into the living room and played with our toys until, exhausted, we retired for a nap. We rested, awoke, and then dressed formally for Christmas dinner that was usually served at four o'clock in the afternoon. After we had eaten, the table was then re-laid. My mother took over and the servants were seated. Dad said the grace and thanked them for their service during the year. We served them their dinner exactly the same way they had served us. After dessert they received their gifts and gratuities. This is one way our parents instilled in us that people, no matter how humble their status, were to be treated with courtesy, respect and dignity. We have tried to observe that throughout our lives. As Claire and I look back we realize that multiethnic Guyanese cuisine was evident throughout Christmas day. It began at breakfast with very local dishes, and ended with dinner in the British tradition of roasted meats, baked ham, roasted potatoes, English fruitcake and trifle deserts. Throughout the Christmas season native and environmental influences were represented on our tables. Root vegetables of various types, plantains, tropical fruit salads, pepperpot along with local drinks and Guyanese rum were always available.

View of Stabroek Market

Traditional Guyanese Pepperpot Recipe

2lb. Chuck beef, and short-ribs or brisket cut up into 2 inch pieces

1/2 lb. corned pigtails cut up

2 pig feet cut up or one cow heel

2 lb. of oxtails cut up

1 cup casareep (a cassava product from Guyana, now found in Asian markets)

2 hot red peppers

A piece of dried orange or lemon peel & a stick of cinnamon

3 heads of clove, 2 oz of sugar and salt to taste

Directions:

Clean all meat well, dry and set aside. Cover pig feet and cowheel with water, boil and skim. When half tender, add more water to cover remaining meats Cook for an hour. Add all other ingredients and simmer until all meats are tender. Serve hot over rice. Pepperpot is best served the second or third day, and must be boiled up every day. This dish is the contribution of the Amerindian peoples, who live in the interior forests of Guyana.

It amazes us now to recall that everyone celebrated this Christian holiday in some form or another. Hindus and Muslims, without violating any of their religious tenets, joined with their Christian friends for dinner and attended parties of the season.

THE MARTIN CHRISTMAS

Christmas celebrations at the Martin home were very similar to those of the Matthews home except we attended midnight mass at Brickdam Roman Catholic Church on Christmas Eve.

Circa 1946-The Martin family at home

I made our Christmas tree the same way Paula made hers. We decorated with blown glass handmade ornaments collected over the years from our grandparents and those our parents brought back from their travels abroad. Celebrating the arrival of "Father Christmas" was a grand affair at the Martin home. We three children spent hours and hours deciding on our list of presents for members of the family and friends. We also had to be careful how we spent our Christmas allowances.

Our mother being a caterer, food preparation and presentation was of prime importance in the Martin household. Mom made the menu for the days of Christmas week and went over it with Miss Marion, our cook. She wanted Miss Marion to know where certain products could be purchased and what dishes would be prepared for each day. Knowing where to get the best cuts of meat for pepperpot, garlic pork, roasts, and ham were all part of the work of gathering and preparing.

My mother placed her orders with Bookers for New Zealand lamb and mutton weeks in advance of Christmas. This planning was also done for standing roasts and cuts of stewing beef and imported ham to make sure she got what she wanted. Butter, jellies, jams and other preserves from Australia and England were also on the list to get from Bookers and Sandbach Parker stores located on Water Street in Georgetown.

Mummy went herself to Stabroek Market to order her ground provisions such as cassava, eddoes, yams and sweet potatoes, as well as fish and other foods from local merchants. I remember going with her and the excitement of moving among her favorite vendors, and the respect and courtesies they extended to her. Some of the older vendors remembered her from "government house days," and of the years she was a teacher at the Carnegie Trade Center in Georgetown.

Stabroek Market Square, Water Street, Georgetown, B.G.

Stabroek Market
Georgetown, the capital

Christmas dinner was always an elegant and festive occasion in our home. We children dressed in our best bib and tuck.

The dinner table was decorated for the occasion with a fine lace and damask tablecloth and napkins to match. English stemware, Sheffield flatware with mother of pearl or bone handles and Royal Doulton dinnerware completed the place settings. Serving platters with rib roasts, baked ham and the like were beautifully garnished and presented. Our father lit the candles on the table just before we were summoned to dinner by the tinkle of a bell. We said grace to remember the Christ child's birthday and then dinner was served. The menu was grand and we were allowed to eat "to our hearts' content."

Here follows a typical Martin Christmas dinner menu:

Meats: Roast capon or turkey stuffed with herbed breadcrumbs and imported chestnuts. Baked ham with a honey orange glaze, whole cloves and Bing cherries in scored squares. Pepper pot made from short ribs of beef, cowheel, corned pigtails and oxtails and a fish dish of some kind.

Side Dishes: Potatoes au gratin, peas and rice cooked in the milk of the coconut, boiled yams, fried yellow plantains and pearl onions in a white butter sauce.

Vegetables: Butter beans, callalou (spinach), bora beans, carrots and green squash and okra.

Salads: Imported canned pears or peaches in aspic, lettuce with slices of cucumbers, radishes and tomatoes served with homemade salad dressings. There were small side dishes of pickled corn, gherkins, pickled beets, and lemon and lime rinds also pickled.

Desserts included English trifle with hard sauce and Guyanese black cake wrapped in marzipan, frosted and decorated by our mother. This was generally served with coffee, a delicious Malmsey Madeira or English sherry or port. We children were allowed coffee- flavored milk, and, as we got older, we were able to partake of real coffee and a small quantity of the "spirits" served to the grownups.

When it was time for dessert, we children got the attention of our parents and other grownups at the table to boast about the presents we opened earlier in the day. The day ended with full stomachs, listening to the BBC on our short-wave radio, playing with our presents, reading new books we received for Christmas and being generally satisfied with our bounty of gifts.

As Paula and I think back to those times, the glowing memories of school mates, dear friends, and family members, many of whom we have not seen since we came to the United States, return to us. We wish that we could remember and articulate all the various adventures and fun times with family and friends shared during those first nineteen years of my life in a colony called British Guiana on the coast of South America. And now let us move on to the next holiday.

Vintage Christmas Tree

Chapter IV

Boxing Day
Claire

The day after Christmas was also very exciting and is called Boxing Day in the British tradition, which was another time for celebrations in the days of our youth. In our family, Boxing Day meant saying thanks to those people who worked for us as well as visiting with relatives and friends and exchanging gifts. Also on this day there would be a traditional local boxing contest, which I was neither allowed nor cared to attend.

"The American Heritage Dictionary of the English Language," 3rd edition, describes Boxing Day as the first weekday after Christmas that is celebrated in the British Commonwealth all around the world. British Guiana was a part of this political structure. The Martin family had much to be grateful for and we showed our gratitude to those who served us over the years of my childhood.

Our parents made sure that we expressed our appreciation.

Some of these persons that I remember included our nanny, who tended to us as infants and until I was about 5 years of age. Miss Marion, who was our cook for over 20 years, and who came to the United States to take care of my brother Christopher's two sons, Deryck and Michael, during their infancy.

I also remember Miriam, a Barbadian immigrant to British Guiana, a wonderful person, and a fantastic maid, who my brothers teased mercilessly because of her very thick Barbadian accent. I remember Ali, our gardener in Essequibo, who tended the milk cow and the acres of fruit trees and the various gardens my mother cultivated. These gardens, with Ali's help, provided all the fresh green vegetables, fruit or ground provisions needed by our household during our five-year stay in Essequibo.

The gifts we gave on Boxing Day ranged from money, clothes, special food baskets and household items, to a day off or all of the above. I remember giving hand sewn–embroidered handkerchiefs, tray doilies and/or money from my allowance. Yes, Boxing Day was indeed a great day to say "Thanks" to wonderful people.

On this day many families included "open house" visits between family members and friends, often to exchange gifts.

Going to our grandparents, Constance & Conrad Martin, was always the best. We particularly looked forward to enjoying special ice creams, pepperpot, cut okra and sweet shrimp and sweet desserts made by Miss Leticia, who cooked for my grandparents.

She made a special ice cream for my grandfather from the ripe soursop fruits that she harvested from a tree which grew in my grandparents' yard.

I was too young to appreciate the need to get a recipe. The following recipe is from my sister-in-law, Ruth Harry Martin, Anthony's wife, who cooks authentic Guyanese dishes.

Claire, Christopher and Anthony
At Grandparents' home – 224 New Market Street, Georgetown

Soursop ice-cream Recipe

4 pints of milk
1 very ripe medium large soursop fruit
4 eggs
2 cups sugar (less or more depending on taste)
1/4 tsp. almond essence
2 oz. custard powder

Prepare the pulp from the ripe soursop fruit by breaking the fruit into pieces, and scooping out the white meat from the green outer skin. The meat has black seeds that must be removed. After this take the white seedless soursop pulp and put it aside. Heat 1½ pints of the milk and pour over the pulp. Put through a large sieve and put this pulp aside for later use. Blend the custard powder in 4 tablespoons of cool milk to a smooth consistency. Heat the remaining 2½ pints of milk in a saucepan to just boiling and remove. Add the custard mixture and blend well. Return to heat until it begins to thicken. Remove from the heat. In a separate bowl, whisk the eggs and sugar lightly and gradually add the almond essence while stirring the mixture. Now gradually add the thickened custard. Whisk well together. Add the soursop pulp and mix well. Taste for sweetness. Let mixture cool and you are ready to make your ice cream. Of course in those days the ice cream maker was churned by hand and we children would sometimes take turns doing this. This participation gave us first dibs at tasting from the churner when Miss Letitia, our maid, took the churner out to serve. Paula has sketched what the ice cream machine consisted of by showing the different components.

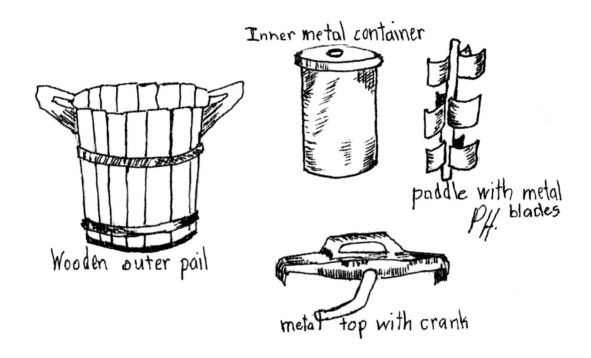

Inner metal container

paddle with metal blades

P.H.

Wooden outer pail

metal top with crank

Old Fashion Ice Cream Machine

The ice cream machine had two containers. The outer one was made of wood and looked like a wooden pail. The inner one was made of metal. A paddle was placed into this small container to churn the mixture. The mixture was poured into the metal container, a cover attached and a device with a crank anchored the whole mechanism. The space between the metal can and the wooden container was filled with layers of salt and ice. The ice-cream making then began with someone turning the crank until it became too stiff to turn, the cream was ready. You can still find a similar ice cream machine today in certain catalogs.

One of my grandmother's favorite dishes was sweet shrimp and okra. Miss Leticia made it for me as a treat whenever I visited after school or on holidays. I am really happy to pass on to you children my Grandmother's recipe for this delectable dish that I often make.

Sweet shrimp & okra Recipe

1 lb. small sweet shrimp peeled
1 onion chopped up
1 lb. fresh okra cut into ½ inch pieces
1 clove garlic chopped finely or pressed
A pinch of fresh thyme leaves crushed or chopped
4 tablespoons olive oil
Salt & black pepper to taste

In a heavy skillet, heat the olive oil until hot. Quickly throw in the okra, onions and garlic to brown, turning often to prevent burning. Add thyme, salt and pepper to taste. Then put the shrimp in this mixture and gently turn all ingredients to mix together. Simmer for about five minutes. Serve over white rice. *Delicious!*

In remembering those times in Guyana, I asked some members of my family, as well as some of my parents' dearest friends, who now live in the United States, to share their remembrances. It was delightful to collect their musings about Mummy's culinary skills and some of the dishes she prepared and served for our "Boxing Day Open House."

Some of these included delicious finger foods of boneless, skinless sardines on delicate squares of buttered crust-less toast, garnished with slices of pickled onion or sweet gherkins. Stuffed eggs in which the yolks were combined with sharp mustard and finely grated English cheeses and horseradish were also a favorite. These were served garnished with a small sprig of parsley and pimento-stuffed olives and sliced into quarters. Sometimes the garnish was delicious caviar, sometimes shrimp, etc.

My brother, Christopher, has inherited our mother's talent for preparing and presenting food in the most mouth-watering ways with flourish and panache. Both Anthony and I are cooks also and have inherited some of our mother's talents. Drinks of all kinds, both alcoholic and non-alcoholic were served in crystal glasses. Some of the non-alcoholic beverages we enjoyed over these festive Christmas holidays were made from local fruits, among them, sorrel, tamarind and five-finger (five-star). These drinks are made very simply from steeping the fruit meat or pulp in boiling water. Take the pot off the burner, add herbs and spices, and let stand overnight. Strain off the liquid and add sugar to taste. If the flavor is too strong, dilute by serving over ice or add water.

Ruth Harry Martin preparing Guyanese dish

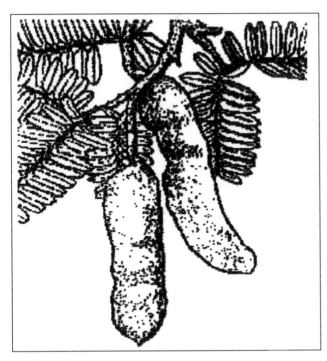

Tamarind Fruit
(Sketch by Paula)

Five-finger drink (Five-star fruit)

5 five-star Fruits (available at large supermarkets)
1 stick cinnamon
2 pieces orange peel
5 cloves

Cut up fruits and boil quickly in a quart of water. Add 1 stick cinnamon, 2 pieces of orange peel and 5 cloves. Let stand until cool. Sweeten to taste.

Tamarind drink Recipe

This drink can be made from the tamarind syrup that is available in Asian and Caribbean grocery stores. Follow the directions on the bottle.

A bonus for us children, on the days of Christmas week leading into the New Year, was the delicious leftover desserts that we looked forward to snacking on until they were gone. In British Guiana from the late 1940s to the late 1950s, we children looked forward to the New Year celebrations with great anticipation. There would be wonderful foods for dinner, midnight mass on "old year's night" and parties until the early morning for the adults. When these parties were held at our home, we were able to participate until midnight, and then off to bed, leaving the grownups to their jollification.

Chapter V
Ring out the Old, Ring in the New
Paula

Claire has told you about Boxing Day, I will try to pass on some of the excitement of New Year's Eve and New Year's Day.

The dawning of the New Year was, as it is today, a time to make resolutions with the hope of bettering one's self and one's situation. But as children, my brother and I looked forward to the spectacle of the changing year.

My father had told us that as the New Year came in, the clouds of the dying year would roll over and hide the moon. The reappearance of the moon heralded the arrival of the New Year. We believed him and rushed out from midnight service to gaze skyward. We were never disappointed, because somehow it happened just as Dad had foretold.

Smith Memorial Congregational Church, Georgetown

It seemed that on cue at our Congregational Church in Buxton, and later at Smith Church the attendees proceeded outside for the final hymn and the New Year prayer. The church bells throughout the village rang, "out with the old, and in with the new." There was then a great deal of jollification and good wishes were exchanged as the church members left for their homes.

At Arundel manse, Buxton, that's when the excitement began for our family. My Dad had instituted a custom of bringing the deacons of the church home for midnight supper. This was an elaborate affair at which the main attraction was a roasted suckling pig. Dad had been introduced to this custom during his student days in London. So each year we had a suckling pig. It was usually the gift of one of the parishioners, who had chosen it with great care.

I loved to watch the cook prepare the beast. She scrubbed, washed and rinsed it several times, inside and out, until it reached her standard of cleanliness. Then she seasoned it, inside and out, with fresh thyme leaves, limejuice and black pepper, rubbed it thoroughly with these and other seasonings, and finally placed an apple in its mouth. It was ready for baking and looked exactly the way we saw it in

British pictures of Christmas feasts. The poor thing was then placed into an open pit of red-hot coals in the yard and left to roast until the skin was crisp and golden brown. This seemed to take forever. The houseboy was assigned to watch it and stoke the coals so that the pig cooked evenly. Wilkins, our cook at that time, was very strict about this process and she would "box" (slap) his ears if she found him inattentive and allowing the skin of the pig to burn. We went to help him "keep an eye," but I am sure we were more of a hindrance than a help to him, since the unfortunate chap had to keep us away from the hot coals and heat.

At midnight, we returned from church to see the beautifully laid table and the pig standing on the sideboard with the apple in its mouth, frills of white paper wrapped around its legs, and the platter garnished with slices of roasted apples, tomatoes and roasted Irish potatoes. The deacons accompanied Mom and Dad. Dad began the proceedings. He blessed the meal and raised a cheer to the New Year by clinking glasses filled with Bulmer's Woodpecker cider. Many of the deacons made a wish and a little speech and then all sat down to the feast of suckling pig, calaloo soup, baked Irish potatoes, rice, cassava cakes and topped off with trifle for dessert, local drinks and a tot of brandy. At this time, my brother Marc and I were excused from the table and scurried off to a small room, off the dining room, from where we viewed the 'goings-on.'

Aunt René Willock, age 93, Baking Xmas Cookies

This recipe for **Trifle Dessert** was given to both Claire and me by one of our mothers' dearest friends, Mrs. René Willock (Aunt Rene'):

1 pound cake, sliced and put aside
2 different colors of Jell-O made according to box instructions
and jelled to a soft consistency. Keep each color separate.
2 pints of custard sauce
1 medium jar of strawberry jelly
1/2 cup of chopped walnuts
1 cup of Madeira or sweet sherry wine

Using a glass bowl, line the bottom with slices of pound cake spread liberally with some of the strawberry jelly. Pour a ¼ cup of sweet Sherry or Madeira wine over this first layer. Then spoon some of one color of the medium set Jell-O to cover this layer and then pour enough custard over this to cover well. Do the same procedure again until all the ingredients are used. Then pour the rest of the wine over the entire dessert and sprinkle the walnuts on top. Keep refrigerated until ready to serve. This dessert may be served with Whipped cream or by itself.

I look back at those times and will always remember my mother as the most beautiful and gracious hostess as she was until her 80s. She had very regal posture and the warmest smile you would see. She was sensitive to the needs of others and did her best to be helpful. To this day I picture her sitting opposite Dad and beaming her soft smile at everyone and at him. She had a wonderful capacity to make everyone feel at ease and her parties proceeded with great love and fellowship.

Una Matthews

We went to bed in the wee hours of New Year's Day, exhausted and happy. As we grew older, we were invited to New Year's Eve parties, which we attended after attending church services with our parents. We also went to New Year's Day picnics with our friends.

Mother Sally as seen at a Caribana Parade
in Toronto, Canada

Another feature we loved to see on New Year's Day was the appearance of Mother Sally, a most fascinating spectacle. Legend has it that Mother Sally came out of her house once a year on this day and paraded around seeking alms. Someone, usually a male, fancifully made up and elaborately dressed as an old woman, stalked the neighborhood on stilts and dancing to music of a steel band. His outfit consisted of a colorful skirt over striped knickers while the stilts he walked on were covered in gay colored stockings. He was a sight to behold and he loved the attention, especially if we were allowed to follow him down the street dancing and cavorting to the steel band music. I will never forget being at a friend's house one New Year's Day when this apparition appeared at the window. He played a lively calypso tune on his flute, and then waited for a tip and some refreshments.

Chapter VI

The Lenten Season
Paula

The New Year celebrations came to an end. We returned to school and life reverted to its routine of school, home, school. The rainy season descended and we found ourselves indoors most of the time. We invented new games, played old favorites and got outside whenever we could. Remember that as we grew up there were no televisions, so we had to use our imaginations and create our own entertainment. As February approached, we looked forward to celebrating three holidays. These were Shrove Tuesday, Good Friday and Easter.

These next three holidays were not all public holidays, but those central to the Christian religion. The first occurred in February and was determined by the date of Easter. It fell on the Tuesday before Ash Wednesday and is called Shrove Tuesday.

Each year, we enjoyed a once-a-year culinary delight, "Shrove Tuesday Pancakes." These are the pancakes that Grandma Matthews, Grandma Hazlewood, and Aunt Ruby Martin enjoyed making and distributed to everyone they could find. These pancakes were introduced to Guyanese cooking by Portuguese immigrants, who came to Guyana as potential laborers but soon turned their attention to commercial ventures such as grocery stores. They were mainly Catholics and celebrated Shrove Tuesday as they had done in Portugal. This day is significant because it precedes Lent on the Christian calendar. The custom was that from that day on, for forty days, there was a minimum of sweets, (candies) available to us. We often gave up sweets as a Lenten exercise in self-denial. Well, for children, it was either a tragedy or a badge of distinction for those of us who got through the period without cheating. Anyway, the adults removed as many sweets as possible from the home, and we knew that desserts would be limited, even for my Dad, to fruit and cheese. So on that Shrove Tuesday all sugar in the home was converted into a syrupy liquid into which the pancake batter was dropped, forming these unforgettable pancakes. They were the final treat of the season. Shrove Tuesday pancakes were incomparable treats, anticipated by everyone young and old. I can recall my eagerness when I left for school that Tuesday morning. I sat at my desk, distracted by dreams of my pancakes. I imagined the huge pot boiling on the stove and all the sugar becoming syrup. We were often encouraged to bring friends home, especially those whose mothers didn't make pancakes. Of course I invited my best friends.

At the end of school on that Tuesday we hopped on our bicycles and headed off. We arrived home with great anticipation. We said our hellos, and waited for Mum to call us to have our pancakes. The kitchen and our home were filled with the most aromatic scents of "sweetness." Mum usually supervised the distribution into our bowls. But before she did that, we liked to look in the pot to see the shapes into which the randomly dropped batter had formed as it cooked. We identified many forms, created by our imagination, as they floated in the crystal clear amber syrup. When we had enough looking, Mum ladled the pancakes into our bowls, dripping with syrup. Sometimes we added some fresh squeezed lemon juice to temper the sweetness. What a wonderful taste, from every morsel drenched in this liquid. Sadly, the ritual came to an end and we continued our routines of life.

Lent meant that life was somewhat altered for forty days and forty nights-the duration of time Christ was in the wilderness. We had to show self-denial. We decided what we would give up for Lent, such as going to the movies or to parties, or our favorite dessert. We were also encouraged to do something constructive, for example, visit older people, help in the home, or make something. We played quiet games at home and read a whole lot more. My Dad always provided new magazines, comic books, and puzzles for our enjoyment. We now looked forward to the end of Lent, ushered in by the solemnity of Good Friday and the joy of Christ's resurrection on Easter morning.

My Mother, Una Matthews, related the following memory of Good Friday she had experienced in her youth. She tells us that, "Good Friday was the most solemn day of the Passion weekend. It was a day of mourning by Christians as they remembered the Crucifixion and the seven last words of Christ on the cross. Appropriate music on the local radio set the atmosphere for this day of mourning. In Guyana and West Indian Islands, men wore dark suits and women and children dressed in white, purple, gray or black. Most people attended church services during the day. All commercial businesses were closed."

As you can imagine, we did not relish Good Friday for it seemed long, boring and too solemn. But there was compensation, yet another annual treat. That morning, we awoke to the cries of a local vendor, "hot cross buns, hot cross buns, come and get your hot cross buns, one a penny, two a penny, hot cross buns." She arrived at the back steps of the kitchen, dressed in her immaculate white dress, her head neatly tied with a stiffly starched head kerchief. She balanced a basket filled with buns and covered with a snow-white towel. We children scampered down the steps to purchase ours. The spicy smell of these buns, with their sugar marked crosses, is unforgettable. We ate as many buns and cheese as our mother would allow. This repast satisfied us until sunset. We ate fruit as the day wore on. We attended noontime service, which traditionally lasted three hours. We were expected to stay for the first hour, during which time the children's story was told. We were then excused and could go home. As I grew into my teens, I elected to stay for the whole inspiring service. In the evening we broke our fast and at sunset, we ate a light meal of fish and cou-cou, a Barbadian dish.

We found this Good Friday meal to be delicious.

Cou Cou

4 fresh okras
1teaspoon salt
2 cups water
1cup cornmeal
1 tablespoon butter
Handful of ham, bacon or any other
cooked meat

Directions:
Cut okras into 1/2 inch slices, or use 1 box of frozen okra. Bring water to boil, add salt and okra Continue to boil until okra is cooked and soft. Add meat. In a mixing bowl combine corn meal with 3/4-cup cold water to make a loose paste. Slowly stir paste into the boiling mixture with a wooden spoon. Continue to stir until the mixture is thick and smooth. Remove from heat and continue vigorously stirring for a few minutes until the mixture coats the spoon without dripping. Spoon into buttered mold, allow to cool. Turn mixture onto platter and serve with stewed beef or fish.

The following day was Holy Saturday, which precedes Easter Sunday. It seemed the world awakened and a big bustle began, although it was still a solemn time and we could not play any loud games, nor did the radio station change its mournful tunes. Actually we looked forward to hearing the music of Bach and Handel.

Kite flying at the Sea Wall
(Sketch by Paula)

Our main occupation on Holy Saturday was the preparation of our kites for Easter Monday morning. Everyone made his or her own kite. In our case, the houseboy was the maker. We chose the colors and Dad provided the crepe paper, while Mom gave us the cloth to make the tails. Together with the houseboy's help, Marco and I made our kites.

The adults had their own activities which included the cook preparing for Easter Sunday dinner and Mum getting the clothes ready. We children always wore new clothes from head to toe for Easter service. Dad was closeted in his study preparing one of the sermons for which he was noted throughout the country. Our meals on Holy Saturday were light and more often than not, we had salt fish cakes for breakfast, pepperpot and plantains for lunch and the last meal could be cook-up rice.

Claire and I discovered that the second most popular holiday among our family and friends was Easter Sunday. They all recalled it as a gastronomic pleasure second only to Christmas. In the Matthews household the day began with a light breakfast as we hurried off to service. It was usually boiled or fried plantains, stewed codfish or some pepperpot with freshly baked bread and a fresh fruit salad. We entered church, very much aware of our new clothes, and sat patiently through the service. I liked to sit in our pew in a position to see what was going on outside. Remember this is a tropical country and the doors and windows are always open. I looked out and saw everything going on. Sometimes I understood most of the sermon and I loved the hymns of Easter. I felt all the emotions of the risen Christ in my own childlike fashion. We stood around after church and greeted our friends until the adults were ready to go home. We went home to dinner around one o'clock.

We came to dinner in our "church clothes," symbolizing the importance of Easter. The first course was hot soup. Dad would say the prayers as the steam rose from our soup plates. Fortunately, Dad was a good soul and made the blessing a brief one.

As we ate, we conversed about the meaning of Easter as well as our plans for Easter Monday. Dinner proceeded. Mom rang the dinner bell as we finished each course and the maid brought in the next one. The main course in most homes was baked ham, turkey or a roast of beef accompanied by ground provisions, such as yams, cassava, plantains, and naturally rice of some kind. The green vegetables served were sautéed tomatoes, fresh sliced tomatoes, bora beans, calalu and/or cucumbers.

When roast beef was the center of attraction, it was served with Yorkshire pudding - a true English menu.

Yorkshire Pudding Recipe

Ingredients:
1/4 cup of the liquid drippings from the roast
2 eggs
I cup sifted flour
1 cup milk
1/2 teaspoon salt

Directions:

Preheat oven to 450 degrees. Beat eggs with cup of milk. Take a cup of sifted flour and 1/2 teaspoon salt and mix into the egg and milk mixture. Beat well. Using 1/4 cup of the drippings from the roast, pour into hot bake dish with the pudding mixture and bake for 10 minutes. Reduce oven heat to 350 degrees and bake for another 20 minutes or until puffy and golden brown. Cut up and serve immediately with slices of the roast beef.

Now dessert, which you will remember we had to forego for forty days, reappeared. Dad's favorite part of the meal was dessert. It was always something that he requested. The rest of the family liked this because he asked for good stuff like brandy fruitcake, snow pudding, baked custard and flaming baked bananas. As an additional treat we might have homemade ice cream. I liked guava ice cream best.

We changed into our play clothes and completed our kites. We could not have a trial run to test our kites. The raising of the kites symbolized the Resurrection of Christ on Easter Sunday. But we had to wait until Easter Monday morning, which was a public holiday, to recognize the occasion.

So welcome to Easter Monday! We were always so excited that we barely ate breakfast, which was an ordinary one. Most likely we had eggs and bread, and maybe fruit and hot chocolate. Our minds were really on kite flying and surrounding activities.

Uncle Bert Harris, a friend of Claire's parents, describes the day this way: "Easter Monday, all the families and youngsters met on a picnic for kite flying, sharing jokes and rollicking amidst the tears of little ones whose kites did not make it into the sky. We would cheer for those kites that succeeded and soared into the air after some adult had added or adjusted the rags that formed the tails of the kites. When there were no rags available, we often used broken pieces of bushes as a substitute. Once the children were happily flying their kites, parents would socialize, toasting their successes with rum and ginger, mauby or other cool drinks from the picnic baskets."

Grandma Matthews added to her Easter remembrances by saying, "Another reason I liked Easter Sunday was that we girls had to have two new dresses, one for church and the other, usually a bright cotton frock, for our Easter Monday kite flying outing. Easter Monday was an exciting day. The women prepared picnic baskets. From early in the morning you saw boys and men with kites slung over their shoulders, families with laden picnic baskets, all wending their way to the seawall on the Atlantic Ocean and other open spaces to raise their kites aloft. The day was spent in kite flying and the opening of picnic baskets. By nine o'clock in the morning, the sky was filled with buzzing sounds and brightly colored objects dipping and weaving about...the kites were flying. For us girls, as we grew older, there were other interests at the picnics. It was an opportunity to be with our friends. We did not focus on boyfriends or girlfriends, just a group of friends of both sexes having a jolly time. That did not mean that we were not aware of a few hand-holdings and admiring looks and comments. How I cherish the memories of the Easters of my youth."

I, too remember my Easter Mondays. We made sure that our kites were very colorful. We were also aware of the evil people who put razor blades on their kite- tails. They flew their kites with the razor blade tails against other kites and by maneuvering them cut the kite string of the victim's, whose kite disappeared into the wide blue yonder. That was really mean, and if the culprits were caught, the villagers banned them from flying their kites in that area. In the city they were chased away from the fields. I also remember the picnic baskets.

Whoa! We'd be starved by noon, having tied our kites to some pole, we gathered around for the treats.

There would be all sorts of sandwiches, meat patties, pineapple tarts, cheese straws, fudge, guava cheese and fresh fruit. My favorite foods were the patties, guava cheese and sorrel beverage. Sorrel is still one of my favorite drinks. The ingredients for sorrel drink are easily available in Asian markets. Try making it for yourself, and I hope you enjoy it as a change from your customary beverage.

As the sun sank in the West we wended our way home, very tired, but ecstatic over our kite's performance, especially if it were still alive and could be flown for a few more days. The next day we would return to school to boast about our Easter holiday weekend. It would be a long time before our next exciting holiday. Our energies would now turn to school performance and examinations.

Sorrel Recipe

1 lb of dried sorrel fruit (can be purchased in Asian or Caribbean stores)
1 teaspoon of grated fresh ginger
1 strip of dried orange peel (about 2 inches)
5-6 cloves
3 pints of water brought to a boil
1 lb of sugar or less to taste
a pinch of grated nutmeg

Directions:

Put all ingredients in a large pot. Pour boiling water into the pot. Simmer for five minutes. Remove from stove and allow to cool. Strain and add sugar to taste. Add a few grains of rice to the drink and leave in refrigerator overnight and serve. Enjoy.

Chapter VII

School bells ring in Essequibo
Claire

Some of the best school days that I remember were spent in a place called Suddie in the Essequibo region of Guyana. It is located at the mouth of the Essequibo River, which emptied into the Atlantic Ocean. This region is a section of the interior. My brothers and I were born in the city of Georgetown and did not really know anything about the jungles of Guyana, as we called the interior. We were 8, 7, and 5, when our father was transferred to this region, and quite happy enjoying our growing circle of friends and attending Mrs. Owen's Preparatory Private School in Kingston, Georgetown. We were sad to leave, but excited about going into the interior and the unknown adventures we anticipated.

Small Native Amerindian Village

Our school in Suddie had beautiful white sand beaches, and our new friends showed us their special games and interests during our morning and afternoon breaks. We were always under teacher surveillance and care. Our schoolmates and my brothers knew that, although the beaches were beautiful and fun to play on, the Essequibo River could be dangerous and we were constantly warned about this. I remember vividly as if it was yesterday, that on a picnic with family and friends, I was playing in a shallow part of the river and apparently the ground dropped off and I went down. I felt myself being pulled under and struggling to get my head out of the water to breathe. I do not know how long I felt myself being carried out away from the beach, and was giving up my fight when I must have raised my head up and saw everyone on the beach waving frantically. Just then, one of our friends grabbed me and swam to the beach pulling me by my arm. I was probably about 10 years old and, since then, I am very respectful of beaches, rivers and oceans.

The Suddie School was a brilliantly painted white wooden, two-storied building. It was large and modern for those times, and the pride of our Headmaster, Mr. Johnnie Brown. Classes were held next to each other in an open plan, but separated and defined by the arrangement of desks, benches, and blackboards. It was not always the best where privacy was concerned, especially when Teacher Slyvanna Isaacs disciplined me by making me kneel on a sandy floor as punishment for some infraction I had committed that day. She was a truly gifted teacher and much loved in spite of her stern disciplinary practices.

During the first nineteen years of my life, Guyana was really quite a wonderful place to grow up.

St. Stanislaus College for Boys

I say that especially because of the adventures we children experienced during the five years we spent in the Essequibo region.

This was also our experience during the years we spent at secondary school in Georgetown. Your fathers, Christopher and Tony, attended St. Stanislaus Catholic School for Boys, and I attended St. Rose's Ursuline Convent School for Girls. During those years in Essequibo, when we were out of school during the month of August, our Dad would take us with him deep into the interior. These trips were part of his responsibility as a Health Officer in the British Colonial Government, and, as I remember, were focused on providing milk and good nutrition information for the poor children and child-bearing women of the region. This seemed strange to me as a child, since we always seemed to have milk in abundance and often heard about the rich farms and cattle ranches of the Rupununi region of Essequibo that supplied the country with dairy products and beef.

Essequibo was a place of many contrasts. Our home was located in the port town named Adventure, several miles from our school at Suddie, and for a year before we attended that public school, we were home schooled by a private teacher who lived in our home. She was the daughter of a very dear friend of our parents (Mrs. Doris McKenzie). Her name was Irma.

We lived among a very large population of the descendants of East Indian and Portuguese immigrants, as well as those descended from Dutch and English colonizers of the seventeenth, eighteenth and nineteenth centuries. I cannot remember meeting any French descendants, although history tells us that Guyana was colonized by the French. We were privileged to meet many Amerindians (the native Carib Indians) when we accompanied our Dad on his trips into the interior. These trips were not without some danger in the beautiful equatorial jungle of the 1940s. Disease-carrying mosquitoes, large and small poisonous snakes, (on land and in the rivers we traveled), and other predatory animals were all around us and fed our adventurous spirits. I remember another incident some years later, when I went with my Dad up a tributary of the Demerara River to visit a mission settlement. The river was overgrown with a vine we called "moka-moka," and one of the boys that drove the launch would have to dive into the river to cut these vines away so that we could continue the journey. Many times the river was teeming with snakes and he was not harmed. In contrast to river dangers, the lakes up in the deep jungle elevations were places where we played as children without fear. Maybe because the native children showed us where they played in these waters in relative safety and we played with them. I remember the Tapacoma and the Ituribisi were the lakes in which we played.

It was in Essequibo that I learned to eat the most remarkable foods of the East Indian population.

My Mom had East Indian cooks and she herself knew of these foods. I was a visitor to their homes, from the wealthy rice plantation families to the poor laborers and servants. Being a rather inquisitive child (a nosey parker), I would ask questions about the food and how it was prepared and cooked. When accompanying my father on field trips to more remote areas and met East Indian families on farms or in small villages, I saw how masala, tumeric, garlic, thyme, coriander seeds and other herbs and spices I do not remember, were ground on a stone by a stone, and used in different ways to season meats cooked in iron pots over wood fires. The different smells were tantalizing and mouth-watering.

Native Amerindian Village in Essequibo Region c 1940

In these remote areas we also enjoyed the hospitality of the native Carib peoples, which gave me the opportunity to see food cooked their way and to partake of their invitations to eat with them. What delicious foods we tasted and what adventures we shared. We saw hunters in loincloths carrying their spears and bringing their kill into the village where the women prepared and cooked the meat from the kill and the ground provisions that they harvested from their fields. We ate labba, wild fowl, wild pig and delicious fish caught in the fresh waters of the two lakes. But it was the foods of the East Indian people that I loved most. One of their festivals that we children enjoyed was Phagwah. It was a Hindu celebration and the best fun was trying to escape being doused with a liquid red dye. You can imagine the variety of foods served that day that I cannot even remember today, but I can see it all in my mind's eye. The best for me were the curries, roti, and daal puri.

Below is a recipe for curried mutton that was a big favorite with our family. You can use lamb.

Curried Mutton (lamb) Recipe

2 pounds of mutton cut into cubes for easy braising
1 large onion diced
2 celery stalks, cleaned and chopped
1 tsp chopped thyme
1 cup coconut milk
2 large cloves of garlic, crushed or finely chopped
2 good size scallions or 1 leek, chopped
4 medium white potatoes, peeled and cut into quarters
4 Tbsp curry powder
4 Tbsp olive oil
½ cup of water
Pepper sauce and salt to taste

In a bowl, rub the cut mutton or lamb with salt and ½ of the garlic, and let marinate for 20 minutes. Cover the bowl. In a large skillet, heat the olive oil over a medium high flame and quickly braise the meat, turning frequently until nicely browned. REMOVE AND SAVE. Turn the heat down to medium and let the pan cool a little. Using the same skillet (do not wash), sauté onions, scallions, thyme, celery and the rest of the garlic until the onion is glassy. Fold the curry powder into this mixture until coated and then slowly add the cup of coconut milk, stirring gently all the ingredients together as they cook. Let this mixture cook for 15 minutes on a low flame and then add the meat, piece by piece, turning each so that the curry mixture coats all the pieces. Pour the juices from the standing meat into the skillet and mix. Add peppersauce and salt to taste. Cover skillet and turn down the heat to low medium and cook for 20 minutes. During those 20 minutes you have parboiled the potatoes and now add them and cover the skillet and cook for another 30 minutes over the same low heat. Periodically check to see if the sauce is getting low and add a little water. Do not make the sauce thin since curry gravy should have a nice thick consistency. Serve over rice or with roti. Choices of vegetables include boiled cabbage, spinach or string beans.

Yes, dear children, Essequibo was a five-year adventure, where my brothers and I acted out the stories of Tarzan, Jane and Boy, along with our dog playing Cheetah. We had large trees in our yard at Adventure, and used rope to swing among those trees with Christopher screaming the Tarzan call we learned from the movies. We even constructed a platform in one of the trees that we called "home". Christopher was Tarzan, I was Jane, and Anthony was Boy. We did eventually grow out of that phase, much to our parents' and our dog's relief.

Our Dad was reassigned to Georgetown in 1949 when we children were at the age where we were ready to enter secondary school. After one year at Main Street Roman Catholic School, my parents sent me to St. Rose's Ursuline Convent for girls, and my brothers to St. Stanislaus College, a Jesuit school for

Circa 1954-55. St. Rose's High School
Ursuline Convent School for Girls.
Mary Sparrock and Claire Patricia Martin,
Georgetown, British Guiana

boys. Being Catholics it was expected that we complete our education in Georgetown under the watchful eyes of nuns and priests. We all three received exceptional education at these schools where discipline and expectations were very high. We entered into this phase of our lives with the knowledge that we were being prepared for attending "university abroad," to become professionals.

Our years in secondary school were eventful, sometimes stressful, but always full of great teachers, dear friends, learning to dance, attending parties, hand-holding and being allowed to go out on dates with boyfriends and girlfriends. For me, our Dad made Christopher attend parties with me as my chaperone. He did not appreciate that role early on, but as his interest in girls grew, he enjoyed teasing me and generally making fun of us all, and having fun himself.

I have not said much about the sports we played. Both your fathers and I enjoyed sports. They were very athletic and enjoyed competitive games. Sporting events were always a great opportunity to have picnics, cocktail parties, and great fellowship with teammates and friends.

At St. Rose's I played a game called 'rounders'. Two teams of girls consisted of pitchers and those at bat. The opposing team fielded the ball hit by the batter. If the batter hit the ball, and it was caught by an opposing team member, that girl was called out. Her teammates on bases had to try to steal in to home plate. This game is very similar to hand ball played in this country. I also played basketball. My team was the Panther Girls and your fathers' team was called The Panthers. What fun! All I remember of my basketball career was that I was so aggressive that I fouled out in several games.

Your fathers were involved in track and field while at secondary school and were outstanding in hurdles and high jump.

Panther girls basketball team, Claire #8, Leila #2

St. Rose's Senior Class - 1954.
Taken at the Kranenburg's home on New Market Street
Georgetown, British Guiana

Claire third from the right.

After graduating from St. Rose's, I had to wait for over a year to get the necessary United States Government approvals to come here to attend college, which I did in 1956. Christopher followed me the next year and then Anthony a couple of years later, after the death of our father in 1958.

Chapter VIII

School Bells Ring in Demerara
Paula

The adventures of a "country" child were quite different from those of a "city" child. Both Claire and I experienced the unique happiness of growing up in the country districts. In 1945, I was awarded a scholarship to attend Bishops' High School in Georgetown. At this time I lived in the village of Fyrish on the Corentyne Coast. The village was about 72 miles from the city of Georgetown. By today's standard that would be a one to two hour trip by car. But in 1945, it took over three hours. The adventure of travelling to the city included a ferryboat ride across the Berbice River in an unreliable boat as well as a slow train ride down the Demerara coastline along the Atlantic Ocean. This trip could not be undertaken as a daily feature. My parents decided that I would reside with some relatives nearer to Georgetown during the school term. This period of my growing up holds a special place in my memory.

Paula on left with friend

There was no other way to get to school than to join dozens of commuters. This commuting began a wonderful lifestyle for me as I made many friends on these trips. I traveled from the village of Beterverwagting on the train and during the time it took for the trip to school and back, we engaged in many activities. We completed our homework assignments and studied for tests. Several of us were often bullied by older students for one reason or another, but managed to hold our own in those circumstances. One of my favorite activities was the intricate system of swapping the pictures of popular film stars of that time such as Lauren Bacall, Greta Garbo and Lana Turner. The aim of these sessions was to fill an album with as many of the admired movie stars as each of us could secure. We had great fun making deals to acquire a certain picture. To make sure that we saw our friends, we learned to board the train at a specific car which we prearranged. Yet, when the train reached my platform, friends leaned out the window and waved madly to identify where they were seated. We made a quick sprint to the appropriate car and hopped on board. There was always great laughter and camaraderie on that train and wonderful friendships were formed and strong bonds of loyalty were forged with my mates. Bonds that still exist today as many of us have remained good friends in spite of living in different countries.

The homeward trip in the afternoon was really special and I looked forward to it on a daily basis. One of my Dad's church members rode this train also. Her name was Mrs. Mercurius and she was a huckster or trader in fruits, sweets and vegetables, as well as other small household items. She was called Miss

Mc. She carried her tray with her, usually on her head. Students purchased her wares. I was treated differently for I did not have to purchase anything. She offered me whatever she liked and I always accepted. I looked forward to her coconut sugar cake sweets best. She always observed whether or not "Parson's Paula" was well behaved and on occasion teased me and cautioned me for speaking too loudly. She reminded us "quiet speech was a sign of refinement". As students at Bishops' High School we were all very proud of our uniform, deportment and good manners. Moreover we knew that we were easily identifiable and could be reported to the school or to our parents. Heaven forbid!

Another pleasant memory of my country childhood and school commuting was the process of transporting my bicycle to and from Beterverwagting on the train. This called for planning skills that I acquired as I organized my actions to assure the accessibility and safety of my bicycle. I did not use it in the village during the week, so it was left in the city for me to use going back and forth to lunch. Each afternoon I left it chained in the racks at school or chained to the racks at the train station, in the event that I had to ride to the station if running late. At week's end I had the bike loaded in a special cargo car of the train. This could be especially challenging. Many times the cargo car was not aligned with the platform. I then had to be very agile and intelligent to figure out, as the train approached, where these alignments would take place. It was exciting to anticipate where to stand and get the bike up to the waiting conductor, who took it from me, whereupon I dashed to get aboard the passenger car before the whistle signaled time to depart. The boys enjoyed this challenge and waited for the last minute to hand their bikes up to conductor and then jumped on the moving train. I recall vividly how nervous I became as I visualized my bike arriving in Georgetown without me and not being there to receive it. As a 12 year old, I found Monday morning's trip an anxious one, but on Friday afternoons I had no such concern since the bikes were always lowered to the ground for us to claim. I was always amazed that Mr. Glenn, the conductor, knew which bike belonged to whom and he never made a mistake as he handed down those bikes, to my knowledge. In the event I was late in getting to receive my bike from him, it was placed on the ground and everyone of us collected our own. It was the honor system and not once did anyone take the wrong bike or was one stolen.

Railway Station, Georgetown, B.G.

In the 1960's the railroads were abolished.

I don't want you to think everything was all sunny. During this time I missed my parents who still lived at Fyrish, and only came to town every other week or so. It was lonely. I missed my little brother, Marc and my cousin, Bernard. Moreover, the kind lady with whom I lived was really "old fashioned". I had to practice the piano every day, as she listened and hurried over if she heard a wrong note. Another thing was that there was no running hot water which meant that when I got up to have my shower at 5 a.m. the water would be dead cold. The shower often didn't work so a bucket of water was brought up from the well and sat in the shower stall. It too was cold. So some mornings were awful and I was glad to catch the train to school.

It was a joyful day when holidays came and I traveled home to my own bed and my loving family. Eventually and fortunately after only one school term my family moved to Georgetown and there was no more boarding out. I came home for lunch every day and to my family, Dad, Mummy, Marc and Bernard.

Chapter IX

Cups of Tea, Scones, and Dainty Treats
Claire

Throughout these recountings of our family, I have written much about the foods we enjoyed. Friendships were also very important in our lives and some of these go back generations and are considered "like family." We Martins have been blessed with having these "like family" relationships. I have mentioned some earlier in these chapters.

When Paula and I discovered that we both wanted to record the culture, food, and kinship ties for our American-born relatives, we asked certain members of both our families' circle of friends to help us remember their involvement with our parents so that we could pass on the recollections more accurately.

Many of your Granny Martin's friends have died, but some are still active and remember their times together. Both relatives and friends contributed to this book and their names and kinship will be a living legacy for you and your children through the coming generations. Their contributions are the stories they tell of specific importance to them, the recipes they shared and what special dishes they learned to make because your Granny Martin taught them or served them during their lifetime. These friends include Aunt René Willock, who was born in Panama. She was married to Uncle George Willock, the editor of The Chronicle, one of the two most important daily newspapers in the country in the 1940s and 1950s. He was a very close friend of my father. The other newspaper I remember is the Argosy. Aunt René is Christopher's godmother. She told me that when Christopher was born, and the midwife announced that the baby was a boy, our Dad fainted and Aunt René had to revive him. She now lives in Boston with her daughter Marcelle, a physician and former Dean of the Charles Drew Medical School. Marcelle and I graduated from St. Rose's together. There are Uncle Bertrand and Aunt Joyce Harris who live in Maryland. Uncle Bertrand was one of our Dad's tennis partners. Other families that were part of our lives included the Collins family, Joan and Rudolph, friends into adulthood, as well as the Lampkins, Sir John Carter–Christopher's godfather–and Uncle of Doreen and Vibert Lampkin. The Burnetts, the Applewaites, the Owens from Kingston, the Taitts, and the Kranenburgs, who lived on New Market Street two houses down from my grandparents' home. We could fill another book of the good times we had growing up with such a caring and nuturing circle of friends who were "like family." Other dear friends who helped to form our characters and have passed on are Aunt Una Matthews and Uncle Pat (Rev. Patrick Matthews) who were friends with my parents before either Paula, Marc or the three of us were born. Aunt Lucille Mendonza Holmes and her husband, Cecil Holmes; Uncle Chappie and Aunt Lucille Hazlewood, Paula's in-laws; Katie Melville Porter's husband, Charles, and her mother, Aunt Lucy Skerrett. And the list goes on.

All these friends were very involved in the social happenings in Guyana during the 1940s and 1950s before I left for college in 1956. Garden parties, cocktail parties and special occasion parties were regular occurrences. The most elegant ones were held during the months when the weather was bright and the heat was not exhausting. According to Mummy and Aunt Rene, those held at Government House, were the last word in colonial elegance. This was during the time of George VI, the father of the present Queen.

For afternoon tea parties, women wore elegant hats and gloves and men wore business suits. For formal evening affairs, women wore long gowns and fancy gloves, and men were in tuxedos and cummerbunds. Mummy told me that the Governor wore full military regalia depending on his affiliation and breeding, i.e., if he was a member of the British peerage or had been elevated by the Monarch.

Those Government House parties that were supervised by our Mother gave her many opportunities to meet many British people of the aristocracy. She met Edward VIII, a grandson of Queen Victoria, known as the Duke of Windsor who abdicated from the throne in 1936, the year of my birth. She also met Sir Anthony Eden, who at one time was the Prime Minister of the United Kingdom; and the Earl of Athlone, whose wife I met as a child of probably six or seven and remember vividly because she asked me about being a member of the Girl Guides. I was not, but became one in my teenage years.

Your grandmother, Ruby was the first Guyanese-born professional woman of color to manage the British Governor's House in British Guiana in the 1920s and 1930s. Her influence was felt not only because she was an outstanding manager, a creative caterer and presenter of food, but because of her unusual selflessness in sharing her talents with many other Guyanese. She influenced the hiring of many Guyanese. As chief of all the household staff, except those under the Aide-de-Camp to the Governor, your grandmother created and managed budgets, oversaw the importation of foods and wines from overseas, managed the groundskeepers, and all other necessary activities that went with her position in those colonial days.

Tea Party

Chapter X

May Day Remembrances
Claire & Paula

Claire

As young children we always looked forward to the month of May and May Day celebrations because we got to enjoy ourselves along with the grown-ups. Festivities included games and wonderful foods such as Dundee cake, home-made ice-creams, finger sandwiches, small meat patties, tarts of all kinds filled with different fruit preserves and May-pole dancing. It was really something special to have the May-pole party at your home and invite all your friends. Our parents did that only twice that I can remember and I was probably only between the ages of 3 and 7. But other parents in our circle of friends held May-pole parties and we were invited. However, for the most part, May-pole parties and dancing were held in playgrounds by the Sea-Wall with the Atlantic Ocean as our background. Growing up with this very English custom was a part of our heritage.

The May-pole was made from a thick post that was stuck in the ground. It was festooned with different colored ribbons attached from the top and flowed down as streamers. We children would be called together by our nannies to gather around the May-pole and take hold of one of the colored ribbons. I remember us girls dressed in our best dresses of chiffon, sharkskin or voile with smocking or embroidery and worn with big colorful sashes tied around our waists in big bows in the back. The boys, my brothers included, wore blue serge, sharkskin or gabardine short pants with neatly pressed white shirts and ties, with knee high socks and shining black shoes. The girls wore frilly socks with black patent leather mary-janes.

As we got ready to dance, we were always reminded that each of us had to go in the same direction with one of us passing under the ribbon streamer of our friend next to us and on the outside of the next so that we ended up weaving the May-pole. We had a lot of fun getting the sequence mixed up and when the music stopped, getting back into the correct cadence and starting over. The boys were usually full of mischief and sometimes tripped us girls or moved too fast or too slow and therefore destroyed the flow of the dancing. Often times they were made to behave by threatening them with losing out on dessert.

May-pole Dancing
Drawing by Paula Hazlewood

After we had our fill of dancing, all the nannies would call us all to our picnic. Blankets were spread on the grass and picnic baskets were opened and we all enjoyed the delicious varieties of food. The next treat we enjoyed after our picnic was attending the musical concerts given by the Military Band that were held in either one of the two beautiful public gardens, Botanical or Promenade, in Georgetown. We would sit around the Bandstand on wrought-iron benches or lay out on the grass in the center of the gardens and listen to music. Just before sundown our nannies would gather us up and proceed home. This wonderful tradition has left many wonderful memories that have remained with me these many years.

"Left, Right, Left, Right, marching along we go"

I, Paula remember my fascination with the celebration of May Day and the plaiting of the Maypole with my friends. This event was so intricately tied in with our British heritage that we adopted it without realizing its peculiarity to Great Britain and the significance of spring. What did we know about spring? In British Guiana there were the "wet or rainy season" and the "hot or dry season." The entire British Empire celebrated May Day, so we were emotionally tied to a tradition of which a long deceased Monarch, Queen Victoria, was the benefactor. It was her birthday that we celebrated with such pomp and ceremony. I recall that as children we sang the following ditty in broken English in fun:

The 24th of May is the Queen's birthday
All al'ya chil'ren laff and play
Jump in the line an wine ya body in time
Yeh! Yeh! Yeh!

We celebrated with a grand march through the main street of our village. The majority of the village engaged in mock military maneuvers, saluted the British flag and marched by for inspection by the sitting British Governor or his representative.

During those years of being involved as a Brownie and later as a Girl Scout, I enjoyed these celebrations. Later when I became a Ranger and marched up front in these parades and saluted the British dignitaries, I counted these times among my proudest times. My mother's sister, Aunt Iris Leitch, was the leader of one of the Ranger troops; they were reputed to be the smartest marchers with perfect precision as they passed by the reviewing stand. A cheer always went up and my Aunt Iris, who walked with a limp, never missed a step, and always got a special recognition for the best group. My Ranger group was jealous, but I was happy for the Smith Church group led by Aunt Iris Leitch.

At the end of those parades held in Georgetown, we marched onto the beautifully landscaped grounds of Government House where refreshments were served and musical entertainment provided by the Police Militia Band. Maids dressed in their finest white frilled aprons over black uniforms served us from highly polished wooden and silver trays that were piled high with crust less sandwiches and cold fruit drinks of all kinds. Another treat as we left was a small bag of fudge and a sweet bun.

I really liked the coconut fudge and coconut sugar cake the best. It was a glorious occasion enjoyed by young and old.

After the march and treat, we dispersed and went home to rest before we dressed in our fancy clothes to attend the afternoon festivities at which the May pole was plaited. The event was awaited with great enthusiasm. We assembled at the home of one of the family members of our troupe and set off for the YMCA fairground. I never participated in the plaiting of the May pole, but enjoyed seeing the coordinated steps of the dancers as well as the colorful outfits. Here again, we were treated to delicacies for sale, from the picnic baskets of friends and family. We children enjoyed spending our pocket money for those items after which we settled back and enjoyed eating and listened to pop tunes played by the Militia Police Band.

These were such good times for children to grow in and we relished our lives and times during that era.

Bishops' High School
Paula and Classmates
(Paula, second row, fourth from left)

Recalling Days at Bishops' High School - Paula

The Anglican Church founded the school in 1870 as a girls' school to educate the daughters of expatriates in Guyana. They were children of the priests, government officials and sugar estate managers. Native Guyanese were admitted by means of merit scholarships or by tuition fees. On January 1,1943 the school was handed over to the British Colonial Government. At its founding the name Woodside House School was given. In memory of three Bishops who were closely associated with the School it was eventually named the Bishops' High School.

In 1910, the motto, "Labor Omnia Vincit" was added to the official emblem, which featured the Victoria Regia lily.

I entered Bishops' High on a Government County scholarship in 1945.

As I look back on my days as a student at Bishops' High School I am struck by how difficult it is to pick out the significant events. I seem to remember that the years were full of activities both social and academic. Those were the years in which I made my lifelong friends; the friends who are still dearest to me and with whom I am in constant touch.

I enjoyed studying, and reading was my favorite hobby. I also prided myself on being a good Latin scholar and realized early that with Latin as a background I could conquer English vocabulary as well as in later days French and Spanish. I was not very good at oral French but had no difficulty in written French. Languages have always fascinated me and I have tried to keep up my Spanish even now. I was not very fond of science and indeed we had a limited amount of exposure to it. Biology was fun, especially since we had an eccentric mistress who took us scavenging on the seashore looking for sea anemones, lichens etc. Our instructors – mistresses- had no difficulty teaching us as we had been taught to be attentive and respectful, whether we liked them or not. Our parents and the society expected us to succeed and later make our contribution to humanity.

At Bishops', I learned the value of perseverance. I was what you would call a plodder. I had to work very hard to get good grades. Since I was in competition with several members of my class, I learned not to give up but to put all my effort into studying. My dad was a great source of encouragement. He often helped me to study by reviewing my work and commenting while letting me know "you could do it". He made studying fun and bought us all sorts of books to read. I developed a love for reading outside of school assignments.

We learned to respect our school, as a privileged institution whose reputation had to be upheld. So even though we were sometimes tempted to be careless on the street we resisted, knowing someone would either report to our parents or, if in uniform, directly to the school.

During these High School years, between my church upbringing, the school's teaching and my parents' living example, I learned that "privilege requires responsibility." As an example, even though we had domestic help, Marc and I had responsibilities at home. At school I had the responsibility to be a team member for the good of my house, Elizabeth, the Girl Guide troop and for the school in general. At church we helped the younger children and did our part in skits and plays for the enjoyment of others. We learned that to give was better than to receive and were taught to give of our money, talents and goodwill to those in need.

The years were filled with birthday parties and fun outings to the library as well as Girl Guide excursions into the interior and along the coastline of Guyana.

The most enduring aspects of my High School days are witnessed by the fact that I founded the BHSNY Tristate Alumni Chapter in 1989, many years after I had attended, as a vehicle to honor the past and ensure support for future students.

Chapter XI

A Tribute to Freedom
"First of August come Again."
Claire & Paula

Emancipation Day - "First of August come again."
"August Break"

We have heard this chant on August 1st for years as children growing up. Our teachers and parents reminded us that the Emancipation Proclamation, freeing the slaves within the British Empire, was declared on this day. It was a day of much significance and was observed as a public holiday. Those of us of African descent celebrated it with enthusiasm, for it showed respect for the history of our ancestors. The British expatriates were pleased that the "generosity" of their ancestors was noted in these celebrations.

The day began with church bells ringing in the village of Buxton, on the East Coast of Demerara that I mentioned earlier in this book. Neighbors gathered in several places throughout the village and formed a procession accompanied by different church choirs merging and singing as they marched to the beach.

I remember how glorious it all sounded and how joyful everyone was as the procession progressed.

The older women dressed mainly in white dresses with their heads wrapped in lily-white starched bandanas. It is a picture that I have carried with me throughout my life and no matter where I find myself on August 1st, I think of those days and those women.

After the march, we schoolchildren returned to the schoolhouse for lunch prepared by the adults from the village. This was always the biggest treat, as we mingled with friends and tried to make sure we collected our assortment of sandwiches, different fruit drinks such as ginger beer, and our favorite choices of desserts.

August Picnic - Marc, Elsa Harper, Paula and Doris Harper
ride off into the Botanical Gardens

Chapter XII

Bringing in the Crops
Paula

August was a great month for us children who had the fun of celebrating Emancipation Day, being out of school and enjoying picnics and trips into the country. Tropical fruits were in abundance and we had a bounty of fruits to pick off trees. These included sapodilla, star fruit, genip, mangoes, sugar apple and guava. We also looked forward to celebrating the reaping of the harvest.

August 1st marked the beginning of our school break for a month.

All Guyanese delighted in a dish called metagee or metem. It is a relatively inexpensive dish and very nutritious. It originated with slaves and then freedmen who from their farms collected whatever vegetables were ripe at the time and prepared them for cooking in a large pot over an open fire. They caught fish and after cleaning them, added the fish to the pot. The pot cooked most of the day so that its contents were ready for eating when the laborers rested in the shade from the hot equatorial sun. The milk squeezed from grated coconuts was the liquid in which the vegetables, fish and salted pigtails cooked. As children we called this dish "Baby Pot," and it was a wonderful part of growing up in the country during the month of August and during harvest months of October and November.

These good times often occurred when we were invited to the "backdam" away from the village for a picnic. The term "backdam" referred to that strip of land that was farthest from the Atlantic coast, beyond the villages and borders the dense equatorial forests of Guyana. It was a place where we delighted to go to experience the fun of making and eating "Baby Pot."

On the appointed day, usually a Saturday, arrangements were made with one of the farmers to take my friends and me on a "backdam" picnic. Of course this included the much-anticipated "Baby Pot." We dressed in our hardy play clothes and yachting (sneakers) shoes and left very early in the morning while it was still dark. This added to our sense of adventure. Leaving the village behind us, we trekked along the bank of an irrigation trench. Eventually we came to heavy and thick underbrush and came out into clearing where a canoe on a river was waiting for us and which we boarded. Being on the river was so very exciting as we were paddled to the farm. We passed farmers working to make their farms thrive and at the same time keeping the jungle at bay. I always marveled at their fortitude.

Children Preparing for Backyard Baby - Pot

Along the river we saw heavily laden banana and plantain trees and we had fun counting the "hands" or bunches on these very tall and stately trees as we glided along the river. We also passed sugar cane plantations and the lush green foliage of ground provisions such as eddoes, yams and cassava or yucca. When the farmers experienced a good growth year, the varieties of fruits and vegetables were in abundance and we anticipated a wonderful "Baby Pot" and a wonderful picnic.

"Baby Pot" was made in a large iron cauldron, which arrived with us in the canoe. We children were instructed to gather the husks of coconuts, dry branches and a few large rocks to make a fire. The adults took over and made the fire, and as it smoldered, the cauldron was placed on the fire filled to a certain level with the inclusion of salted pigtails and all brought to a boil. We children were directed to choose the vegetables, peel and cut these up for the pot. One of the adults would crack a water coconut, extract and grate the white meat, soak in water and then strain off the liquid called "milk". It was added to the cauldron and flavored the entire meal. After what seemed like an eternity, the pot was ready to receive the vegetables, which we children had prepared. The "Baby Pot" was now in the final stages of cooking and sent up delicious aromas into the air.

We children waited impatiently for the call to eat. In the meantime we played games, picked various fruits off their trees or vines. Finally, we were summoned to eat. Each of us was given a banana leaf that was used as a plate. The meal from the "Baby Pot" was spooned onto the leaf and the feast began. To me this was the sweetest meal. The vegetables were always succulent, the combination of the meats, the milk of the coconuts, and cooked fresh fish, caught in the nearby trench, flavoured the pot. All this made for a fantastic gastronomic experience, which I will never forget.

As our day ended with this feast, we packed our belongings and made sure that the fire was thoroughly smothered. We returned to the canoe for our homeward journey. Tired and sleepy, I returned to my home in the village, took a shower and went to bed happy and contented after a day of adventure in the "backdam."

What was a fun dish for us children was a serious part of Guyanese cuisine and was known as metagee or metem. This dish was served for lunch on Wednesday or Saturday in my own home. My mother never served this dish for an evening meal because the root vegetables were difficult to digest and one needed physical activities after eating.

This was harvest time, as with most civilizations there is a religious aspect to the holiday. The churches all celebrated with a Harvest Service. It is in the tradition of all Thanksgiving from ancient times to this present day.

The Sunday service started with the bringing of the produce, which was laid around the altar decorated with palm fronds, flowers, and plants of all kinds. Special harvest hymns were sung and my favorite was:

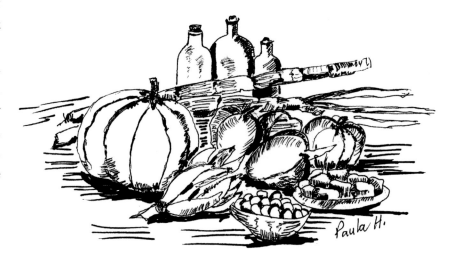

"We plough the fields, and scatter the good seed on the land
But it is fed and watered by God's almighty hand;
He sends the snow in winter,
The warmth to swell the grain,
The breezes and the sunshine,
And soft refreshing rain"

Plaited bread was included in the bounty at the altar, The women molded and twisted the raw dough into intricate shapes and designs representing different fruits and animals and baked the loaves. Fortunately for us, the family of the minister was given many gifts from the harvest, which included loaves of these plaited bread, fruits and vegetables. After the harvest service, these goods were sold to church members and other villagers as a fundraiser for the church. In the afternoon of Harvest Sunday we were usually treated to a musical Penny Concert, so called because admission was a few pennies.

Harvest marked the end of the growing season and provided a respite for the farmers and the land until the heavy rains of December were over. Harvest time also heralded the coming of Advent, Christmas and the New Year.

These events, that we have recounted throughout this book of reflections and recipes, remain with Claire and me, and have helped to weave the fabric of a very rich childhood in British Guiana in the 1940's and 1950's.

Claire & Paula in front of the White House,
Washington, D.C. mid 1980s

Conclusion

The journey is complete; you've traveled with us this far. You embarked and navigated passages through a typical year of our youth in Guyana (then British Guiana). It has been several years since we lived that journey and the 1940s and 1950s are far behind us. The country we lived in has changed dramatically, politically, socially and morally, in the ensuing years. Yet our memories have remained vivid. It was a great time to have experienced our youth.

Writing has not changed our views. We still relish our delicious native dishes. We do create them here in our adopted homeland, U.S.A. As we wrote, some things became very clear to us. First, that one never loses the love of one's birth land; second, family relationships and traditions are of great value and must be preserved from generation to generation. We all know that "times change and we with them" so it is important to leave behind those revelations from the past.

We hope that you enjoyed your trip, and that you will try one or two of the recipes we've provided.

Our quest of communicating to you readers our memories is accomplished. The prize is yours.

The Song of Guyana's Children

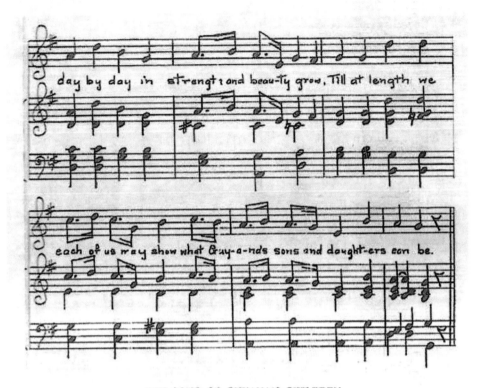

THE SONG OF GUYANA'S CHILDREN

Born in the land of the mighty Roraima,
Land of great rivers and far stretching sea;
So like the mountain, the sea and the river
Great, wide and deep in our lives would we be;

Chorus:

Onward, upward, may we ever go
Day by day in strength and beauty grow,
Till at length we each of us may show,
What Guyana's sons and daughters can be.

Born in the land of Kaieteur's shining splendour
Land of the palm tree, the croton and fern,
We would possess all the virtues and graces,
We all the glory of goodness would learn.

Born in the land where men sought El Dorado,
Land of the Diamond and bright shining gold,
We would build up by our faith, love and labour,
God's golden city which never grows old.

Thus to the land which to us God has given
May our young lives bring a gift rich and rare,
Thus, as we grow, may the worth of Guyana
Shine with a glory beyond all compare.

The Song of Guyana's Children

Born in the land of the mighty Roraima,
Land of great rivers and far stretching sea:
So like the mountain, the sea and the river
Great, wide and deep in our lives would we be;

Chorus:

Onwards, upward, may we ever go
Day by day in strength and beauty grow,
Till at length we each of us may show,
What Guyana's sons and daughters can be.

Born in the land of kaieteur's shining splendour
Land of the palm tree, the croton and fern,
We would possess all the virtues and graces,
We all the glory of goodness would learn.

Born in the land where men sought El Dorado,
Land of the Diamond and bright shining gold,
We would build up by our faith, love and labour,
God's golden city which never grows old.

Thus to the land which to us God has given
May our young lives bring a gift rich and rare,
Thus, as we grow, may the worth of Guyana
Shine with a glory beyond all compare.

Scenes of Georgetown, Guyana

Scenes of Georgetown, Guyana

Scenes of Interior, Guyana

Children of Guyana

Scenes of Guyana's Coastline